INTERVIEW LIKE A PRO

How to stop the self sabotage and get the job you deserve

JENNA KIMBALL

© 2021 Jenna Kimball
All rights reserved.

No portion of this book may
be reproduced either in print
or in any digital format without
express written permission from
the author.

BOOK AND COVER DESIGN
Ryan W. Kimball

TYPEFACES
Futura by Paul Renner
Baskerville by John Baskerville
Univers by Adrian Frutiger

Contact the author at
info@jennkimball.com

Contents

5 **INTRODUCTION**

9 CHAPTER 1:
HOW TO FRAME YOUR EXPERIENCE

    9 The Elevator Pitch

    18 Articulate Your Deal Breakers

25 CHAPTER 2:
INTERVIEW PREPARATION

    25 Should You Do the Interview?

    28 Interview Preparation 101

    29 Interview Preparation 201

    34 Goals for Each Phase of the Interview Process

37 CHAPTER 3:
INTERVIEW SPEAK

    37 Getting the Real Answers You Need on Questions You're Afraid to Ask

    48 How to Answer Typical Tricky Interview Questions

55 CHAPTER 4:
INTERVIEW ETIQUETTE

    56 Corresponding with the Hiring Team

    56 Phone Interview Etiquette

    58 In-person Interview Etiquette

- 59 Thank You Note Rules
- 62 Interview Follow Up

CHAPTER 5:
WHAT TO KNOW BEFORE ACCEPTING AN OFFER
67

- 67 Questions to Consider as You Weigh Your Offer

CONCLUSION
73

ACKNOWLEDGEMENTS
79

ABOUT THE AUTHOR
81

Introduction

You're great at your job. You have a ton of marketable skills. But you're not getting an interview. Or, you got the interview, and you thought it went well, but for some reason, you didn't get hired for your dream job! So what needs to change?

Good news, you've come to the right place. This book will help you get your next job, your first job, or your dream job.

I'm an executive recruiter and have coached thousands of candidates through their job interviews. I am constantly inspired by the talent I meet through these conversations. I love learning about business and helping people connect the dots, and I truly care about people realizing their dreams. Many candidates have asked me to interview for them on their behalf. I think they were joking, but honestly, I wish I could just be a professional interviewer!

Before making the move from marketing into recruiting, I was a candidate who interviewed for lots of jobs. I love interviewing, but I know a lot of people dread it. So I want to equip you with the right tools so you can at least dread it less...you might even get to the point of enjoying it! (I know, let's pace ourselves!)

I have more than 12 years of interviewing experience, both as a candidate and a coach. I wrote this book because I want to alleviate the same problems I've seen in entry-level candidates all the way up to executives:

- People don't know how to frame their experience.

- They don't know how to ask the right questions that yield the answers they need.

- They disqualify themselves or end up in jobs they despise because they didn't know how to show their unique value or what to look for during the interview process.

So I'm going to give you tools, real anecdotes and some tough love/big sister advice on how to prepare and ace your job interview.

A lot of what we are talking about in this book is, of course, developing interview skills, but also working on selling yourself. In order to do that, you have to believe you've got *it*. Sometimes when hiring managers are deciding between you and another candidate, confidence, not skill for the actual job, will win out. If you think you aren't good at your job (maybe you got fired, laid off, had a bad manager, are looking for your first job and don't have experience, etc...) you'll be right. If you show up to an interview without confidence, you might as well wear a sweater to the interview that says, "Don't give me the job."

In this book, I'm going to help you:

1. Create your elevator pitch (a quick summary of your unique value for a specific job)

2. Prepare the heck out of an interview

3. Ask the right questions

4. Follow up strategically

5. Help you decide if you should take an offer

All of that is going to, by default, increase your interviewing confidence. I'm just giving you the bricks, though...you have to build the house.

Let's start building!

CHAPTER 1:
How to Frame Your Experience

Know your potential...and your limits

"Be sincere, be brief, be seated."
— Franklin D. Roosevelt

The Elevator Pitch

Who are you, what are you looking for in your career, and how can you help me, the employer?

I know what you're thinking: "Are we there yet on becoming an interviewing expert?"

I know you've been busy doing your actual JOB, and not cultivating your interviewing skills, which is a completely different thing. So let's start at the beginning.

A somewhat shocking revelation about job interviewing is that it is truly an existential process. I mean, obviously you have bills to pay so you have to work, but what do you love to do? What lights you up and inspires you? What tasks do you enjoy about your work? What makes you good at your job?

Before you step foot anywhere near an interview, you need to know why you are unique and what value you add. You need an elevator pitch—a succinct, informative, tight professional bio that you could rattle off comfortably on a short elevator ride.

I've been an executive recruiter for years and I've interviewed **THOUSANDS** of candidates from entry level all the way up to the executive level. I see two huge mistakes consistently across all levels of experience:

1. Candidates cannot articulate why they are valuable.
2. They know generally why they are good candidates, but don't know how to pick out what's relevant about their experience for a specific job.

So, we need to iron that out right now before we go any further.

Get out a sheet of paper (you can do a word doc on your computer or phone but research shows writing things down by hand makes more of a mental impact).

Write down any notable accomplishments in your career. Here are some questions to get your gears turning:

- Have you managed a team? How many people? What disciplines were they responsible for? What level are you reporting to?

- What size company, revenue and industries have you worked in?

- What kind of revenue have you managed or contributed to bringing into your company?

- Have you won any awards, do you have any certifications, published articles, have you done any speaking engagements?

Those are the basics, but let's also add:

- What are you good at professionally—building teams, hitting sales goals, making processes more efficient, etc.?

- Why do you like/why did you choose the industry you are in?

- Why should an employer pick you over someone else with your exact experience? (What's unique about you, and how is that relevant to this specific job?)

It's important to make an exhaustive list of everything, so you have what I call a "bank" that you can use to pivot between jobs with different qualifications and skill sets.

Now that you have a list of all of these qualifications and your professional passion points, which are most pertinent to the job you're interviewing for? Pick 3–5 aspects that are most relevant for that job.

It is absolutely essential to be selective with what you include in your elevator pitch, because not only does it showcase how awesome you are professionally (obviously) but it shows a recruiter or employer, "Wow! She knows what is really important and will be able to help ME drive what's important to MY business."

Initial interviews with a recruiter or a hiring manager are usually 30 minutes—sometimes even shorter. When the interviewer asks you, "Tell me about yourself", they don't want to hear that you were born on a Thursday in 1994. They want to know what value you would bring to their company, why you are unique and what's in it for them to hire you.

So back to your elevator pitch. Take your exhaustive list and put each qualification in one of two columns:

HARD SKILLS	**SOFT SKILLS**

What's the difference between hard and soft skills?

If I say, "Do you have this experience", and you can easily answer yes or no, that's a hard skill.

Examples could be software programs you know, number of people and disciplines/departments you've managed, industries you've worked in.

Soft skills are more abstract and subjective.

Examples could be good communication skills, highly organized, can pivot quickly with change, strong in a crisis, etc. It's harder to evaluate those, but they are also essential.

Here's an example of what your columns could look like:

HARD SKILLS	**SOFT SKILLS**
Familiar with Python, Google Analytics	Communicated new branding initiatives to team members, resulting in early adoption and minimal adjustment periods
Spoke at XYZ Conference in [year]	Worked with multi-generational team members
Managed teams from 3–7 employees	Can pivot quickly with change
Obtained SHRM-CP certification in 2021	Good at creating processes for new initiatives

For every soft skill you list, think of a specific example that has led to a result. So if a hiring manager asks you about those skills, you'll be able to explain a real-life scenario.

For example, it says here, "Can pivot quickly with change." What does that mean? In an interview, you could say something like, *"We pitched three ideas for our client for a rebranding initiative. After discussing each idea, we combined two of them, and re-did all of the creative and assets in under 72 hours to meet the deadline."* So here you are giving an example of how you were able to roll with the punches, which yielded a successful outcome for all parties.

I bet you wrote down a ton of great skills that you have (we've already established you are amazing).

When creating an elevator pitch, people always want to start at the beginning and speak chronologically. That's a mistake. Don't worry about which year you worked at the job. Pick what's relevant and focus on what you did and why you could do that (and more?) in your next role.

Think of each experience or skill that you have as an individual puzzle piece. Some combinations work for some puzzles and different combinations for others. Your pitch can change for the ears of your audience and it will evolve as you achieve more and advance in your career.

Here's an example of a tight elevator pitch when an interviewer says "Tell me about yourself":

> *I have 7 years of experience building teams and bringing my company from local to national recognition through marketing efforts, and I'd love to do that with you and your company. I am currently the senior most marketer reporting to the CEO of a $80MM recruiting firm headquartered in Atlanta.*
>
> *During my time with the firm, I have built an eight person marketing function from the ground up, which now consists of digital marketing, communications, PR, content and sales operations. This year alone, our marketing efforts drove $500K*

in incremental revenue by driving new client leads into the firm, Amazon being one of them. We have also landed press in Fortune Magazine as a Best Place to Work which attracted over 250 new employees to the firm in the last 2 years.

I love building for-profit marketing teams that drive bottom line results and thoroughly enjoy solving complex business problems through the power of marketing.

Here's why it's good...

→ **He mentions his management experience** and what those employees are responsible for...therefore it's safe to assume he has at least a cursory knowledge of all of those departments. He also mentions he reports to the CEO, which matters, because that can elevate the level of jobs he can be considered for (VP and Senior Director, or maybe even an SVP at a smaller company).

→ **He talks about scaling.** If you have seven years of work experience, that's enough time to have scaled something. Or maybe you've reduced costs and increased efficiency. How did that affect revenue? Some people work at Google or Apple, but outside of that, most people probably aren't going to be familiar with your company's revenue numbers. Use numbers in your elevator pitch for a point of reference.

→ **He mentions results and big wins.** Every employer wants someone with a proven track record. If you have awesome results at your previous company, they will think you are at least capable of repeating them (or even exceeding!)

→ **It's short.** Six sentences. Longer than that, and the listener will lose interest.

Here's why it's great...

→ **The first line sums up what he can do and why the listener should care:**

> *I have 7 years of experience building teams and bringing my company from local to national recognition through marketing efforts, and I'd love to do that with you and your company.*

I've given specific direction here, but maybe not all of that makes sense to share with somebody. For example, if he wants to transfer outside of marketing, scale is important but the specific marketing disciplines are not. In that instance, he should talk more about other transferable skills, like managing a diverse team, driving recruitment and revenue efforts and landing large clients.

Remember to keep your pitch succinct though!

A candidate that rambles on and on is not going to get the job...because, again, they don't know what's important and they are not going to figure out what the company needs to prioritize. I know that's harsh, but it's true.

Please believe me when I say you are amazing. For starters, you have great taste in books!

But guess what? A lot of people are amazing. If you can't explain why your skills are relevant to the job you're interviewing for, someone who can will get that job instead of you (even if your on-the-job experience might be better)!

✎ EXERCISE

Go through your list of skills and write a short elevator pitch. Read that elevator pitch in the mirror. Do you believe you yet? What are some "alternate" puzzle pieces that you can throw in here and there when the time is right? Practice mixing it up. Write it out and write several versions if you need to.

Articulate Your Deal Breakers

So we know you have so much potential, but as the Meatloaf song goes:

I would do anything for love [or employment], but I won't do that…

As you've come up with your elevator pitch, you've articulated what you **CAN** do and where you want to go, but where **DON'T** you want to go?

Before you head to your first round interview, you don't have to have your deal breakers set in stone, but it's important to think about what you need before you accept a job, or what you absolutely are **NOT** willing to do.

For example:

I went through five rounds of interviews for a recruiting job. They were considering me for two roles—one was managing a team, and one wasn't (the pay was lower for the latter, but less responsibility).

They decided to promote someone internally for the manager role, and asked if I would consider the lower level position. I said, if it aligns with what I'm looking for, I would definitely consider it. Managing a team is not a deal breaker for me, but a base level compensation is.

That said, in the end, it didn't work out. The salary range for the lower level role was 20% less than what I had applied for. That's a big difference to me, so I suggested they could help me pay childcare expenses (which were comparable) and I would be fine with a lower base salary. They couldn't do that for me either. So even though I was unemployed at the time, I couldn't take a 20% pay cut plus pay childcare costs on top of that cut.

Another example:

I worked in PR for seven years prior to recruiting. I applied for recruiting roles without specific recruiting experience, but I felt I had a lot of transferable skills. A company gave me an offer that was 35% less than what I made working in PR. I accepted the job, even with the drastic pay cut. It was worth it to me to gain that experience, so I bet on myself. Within a year, I had excelled and was given a large raise and quarterly bonuses which, for the most part, covered that difference. I didn't have aggressive bills or children at the time, so I was able to make that work and it was a great decision.

There are no wrong answers to deal breakers—just YOUR answers. Here are some starting points, but you may ask yourself other questions:

- What is the salary range you really need to cover your lifestyle? Or, are you willing to change your lifestyle if needed? No shame in eating PB&J's every night!

- Do you have a young baby and need to work from home sometimes?

- Do you need health insurance?

- Do you want an environment where most people leave at 5pm everyday?

- Do you want to work at a place where there's a clear ladder to climb or do you want a job that won't change very much over time?

- Are you trying to save aggressively for retirement?

- Do you have student loans or are you pursuing an advanced degree where tuition reimbursement would sweeten the deal for you?

- Do you have unlimited vacation now and are accustomed to planning vacations with autonomy?

I worked for a company that had amazing health insurance and an unbelievable on site gym. But I was on my husband's insurance. Also, the office was an hour from my house and I didn't want to spend even more time at work, so I never used the gym. So when companies hit you with all their "benefits", make sure the bells and whistles are ones you like and fit your needs.

You may want all of these things, and probably other things I didn't name, but what is really non-negotiable? Be honest with yourself here.

✎ EXERCISE

Think through your deal breakers by asking yourself these questions:

1. What are the top 3 things you need in a job? Maybe you've crunched the numbers, and in order to take a job, even if you will love it, you cannot go lower than a certain salary/hourly wage. That's OK. We all have bills!

2. Next, what are 3 nice-to-haves? For example, I LOVE working from home, but I would be OK with going to an office sometimes.

3. What's your biggest deal breaker? Start by saying, "The job is perfect, but..." Example: The job is perfect, but I don't want to drive more than an hour from my home, because I have small kids and I will miss their bedtime.

Remember:

Knowing your elevator pitch and understanding your deal breakers will give you the confidence to make the right decision at offer time (covered in Chapter 5).

You are worth the effort and you only need one offer! You can only take one date to the dance anyway!

So now that you've tightened your elevator pitch, have verbalized your deal breakers, let's prep for your specific interview.

CHAPTER 2:
Interview Preparation

"To fail to prepare is to prepare to fail."
– Benjamin Franklin

Should You Do the Interview?

Everyone gets nervous when they interview…even yours truly! And I've been on tons of interviews as a candidate myself, and I've prepped thousands of candidates as a recruiter. Nerves are OK…not preparing is **NOT** OK!

But first, should you even do the interview?

You wouldn't believe how many candidates cancel interviews last minute. If you're trying to decide, consider these scenarios…

Do the interview:

- It's a first round interview, and a minimal time commitment for both parties

- You've been referred by someone in your network (keep those relationships strong!)

- You're happily employed but you want to know what else is out there. And you want to know if you are compensated fairly

- You haven't had an interview in awhile, so you need to practice - just like any other skill

- You have other interviews, and you want to see how this compares

- You don't understand what this job is or why they called you but you have a microscopic inkling of curiosity

- You have an offer in hand that you're excited about (this interview will confirm **OR NOT** how good the other offer is)

Cancel the interview:

- You've done a few interviews with the company and you don't think it's a good match, and they will be flying you out or investing a lot of time and resources in you

- Emergencies come up. Let the interviewer know with as much advance notice as possible, apologize only once, and offer large windows of time that you can reschedule

As you can see, I lean toward pretty much always going through with an interview, because, well, you never know.

Example:

I landed an internship at CNN about 10 years ago. I was pretty excited about it, and learned there were three teams that I could be a part of within the PR department. I wanted the daytime TV team because that sounded really cool to hang out with CNN anchors, but I was asked to interview for the digital team. I was like, "What? I have to do technology?!?" So I did the interview, and let me tell you, the digital team was so cool. The work was the most exciting, and I learned so much and the people were the best. If I had been too closed off and not considered all my options, I would have missed out on an amazing experience. I loved the team and ended up loving the internship, and was later hired by that same team full time and loved it too!

Another example:

Several years later, I moved cities and was interviewing again. I got contacted by a company to do PR for a high-end dating service. Finding love for millionaires sounded fun, but they wanted me to be in the office everyday and unofficially said that everyone wears a full face of makeup and high heels. As the self-proclaimed inventor of "business comfortable" attire *(patent pending on that phrase) that *kind of formal environment is just not me. Let's just say...when I rushed for a sorority my freshman year of college, I wore tennis shoes when everyone wore dresses. Know your deal breakers!*

Now that you've decided to follow through on the interview, there are a ton of simple and quick things you can do to prepare.

Interview Preparation 101

- Research the company. Are they public or private? You need to know how they make money and understand how their products or services work.

- Know the salary range generally for that type of role. Is that range doable for you? They will ask what you are seeking, so be ready to know the market range for this job. You can find this on a lot of job review sites (ex: Glassdoor, Indeed, CareerBuilder, Salary.com, Payscale.com)

- Go to the company's website and read their "About Us" section. Who is on their leadership team? Read their bios. Are you impressed? Do you have anything in common with them? What do you feel like you could learn from them?

- Check LinkedIn and Glassdoor and other online review sites. Not only will you be able to see the number of employees and reviews of their leadership team, but you'll also see sample questions that people have been asked during their interviews. A lot of times, large companies have a 'question sheet" and they use the same questions over and over again. It's like taking an open-book test—the resources are right in front of you!

If you want to raise your interview prep game, here are some more tips...

Interview Preparation 201

- Revisit your elevator pitch from Chapter 1. How does that line up with what you are interviewing for? For instance, are they seeking someone with industry experience, are they looking for someone who has worked in retail and pivoted into eCommerce, etc...? Where do you fit? Draw the connections and make a note to mention those key points during your interview.

- Read the job description at minimum five times before your interview. Highlight certain qualifications that you know you have and come up with stories around those. If they are looking for someone who has experience with email marketing, note the email platforms you have used and know any relevant stats (how you helped the company increase their open rate, conversion rate, etc. which ultimately led to X amount of revenue/sales)

- If you know who you are interviewing with, look them up on LinkedIn and write down specific questions for them.

We will get to how to ask and answer specific questions in the next chapter. But for now, here are general interview tips:

Particularly for a phone interview, practice your energy. I know that's "hippie-dippie" as my mom would say, but I'm on the phone all day, and I can tell you in less than 15 seconds who is confident, probably pleasant to work with, and knows what they want. They have good energy. I want to talk to them.

Maybe you are more soft-spoken or not a phone talker. Try these:

- Stand up when you're on the phone!

- Smile when you are on the phone. You might look like a weirdo, but they can't see you, so go with it!

- Have your resume next to you...that way, if they ask you something very specific or from several years ago, having your resume at your side will jog your memory. (And you will mentally feel more prepared, which will make you less nervous.)

- Have your list of questions for your interviewer and any key points you want to emphasize right next to you. Don't say to yourself "I'll remember that for the interview!" You won't. The conversation will go a different direction and it will fly by.

- Before the interview, to get your energy in a positive place, do something that makes you happy. Call a friend for a pep talk, watch inspiring YouTube videos (I always watch the Chicago Bulls starting lineup intro to get myself hyped up), go for a walk, or drink some coffee or tea (decaf—you don't want to bring **TOO MUCH** energy!)

If you are interviewing in person or on video, what are you planning to wear? If you check the company's website and social media, or if you talk to the HR team ahead of time, you'll get a feel for how formally or casually you should dress.

My move for an interview is a dark colored solid dress, minimal and understated jewelry, medium heels and dark jacket. I like that because it can feel dressed up or down depending on the environment.

For male candidates, I would recommend an oxford shirt, suit jacket, no tie, and nice dress pants and loafer-type shoes. Know your environment though. If it's professional services (banking, legal, finance, etc...) you may want to step it up to a more formal outfit. If it's an agency or creative environment, you could wear a blazer instead of a suit jacket.

Is your outfit clean/dry cleaned? I had a guy interview with executives and the feedback was that he was "making weird eye contact." I had spent time with him before the interview and he didn't do that in our interactions. Turns out, he had a mustard stain on his pants, and didn't notice until he was in the company's lobby. He was freaked out about it throughout his whole interview. Don't let this happen to you!

Bring copies of your resume.

"They told me they have it."

Bring copies of your resume.

"This is an informal meeting."

Bring copies of your resume.

Maybe I wasn't clear.

Bring copies of your resume.

Even if you never need to pull them out of your folder, interviews can have a spontaneous element to them sometimes, and you need to be ready for anything. I was in an interview and the CEO just walked in to shake my hand. He offhandedly asked for my resume, and luckily, I had extra copies and gave him one.

If you get asked for your resume, and you don't have one, they will assume you are not serious and are generally an unprepared person. So simple, but it says so much about you as a candidate!

Another tip: Have anecdotes ready for common interview questions.

- Think about a time when you've overcome a professional obstacle. Personal (but not too personal) can also work here, but professional examples are generally better.

- Think about a time when you managed a difficult situation, project, employee—highlight the problem and how you found success or learned through the experience. Always end it on a high note. And keep it short (20 seconds or less—time yourself if you want!).

Goals for Each Phase of the Interview Process

Try to get clarification on the interview process as early as possible. Always ask about next steps at the end of an interview. You are subconsciously making them think they want to talk to you again and it shows you are an optimist. I said it before, but it bears repeating: **energy matters!**

First round interview

Know who you are going to be talking to. Is it the hiring manager for the role or the HR representative? You should still have specific questions prepared, but knowing the filter of who would be answering your questions is important in how you ask them. (Questions covered in Chapter 3).

Your goal after a first round interview is to understand what the job is. You can learn about salary, company culture, benefits, etc. later. By the end of a first round interview, you need to make sure you understand as much as possible about the work itself, because if the work doesn't sound appealing, even if they offer you a million bucks, eventually you will dread going to work.

Second round interview

Understand how your role fits into the company's goals, mission, and how your success is judged/measured. If the first round interview is more specific, think of the second round as more big picture. Do you like what you see?

Subsequent interviews

Make Sure: You see the office before you take an offer. If you want to get a sense of work/life balance, see if you can schedule an interview later in the day. Are people really gone by 5pm like the company touts or is that just aspirational?

You **MUST** meet your team or if you are an individual contributor, you must meet a peer. Your peers/teammates will give you a more accurate slice of what real work life is like there. Remember, they want to work with someone they like too.

✎ EXERCISES

1. Practice your energy. Call someone (a friend or family member) and talk to them with your 'interview voice'. Or, record yourself - do you like what you hear? Would you hire you?

2. Go through the Interview Preps 101 and 201 for your interview.

So you're pretty much prepped for your interview except for interview questions. I've got a question for you. What are you waiting for? We cover these in Chapter 3. Let's go!

CHAPTER 3:
Interview Speak
How to Ask and Answer Interview Questions

"There are no right answers to wrong questions."
— Ursula K. Le Guin

Getting the Real Answers You Need on Questions You're Afraid to Ask

Isn't it the worst at the end of the interview when the manager asks you:

"Do you have any questions?"

I'll tell you what's even worse than that—**NOT ASKING ANY QUESTIONS!**

Your overall question-asking strategy should be open-ended and positive.

You want to let HR or the hiring manager do at least half of the talking, if not more.

Wait, aren't they supposed to get to know me first?

No.

NO!

I know I just blew your mind, so I'll wait a second before I make another point.

Initially, they only need to know enough about you and your skills to know if you should move forward in the process. Interviewing is a two-way street. You are really interviewing each other, and you have a lot more leverage than you think.

Remember, they want to hire you. Yes, they do. Let's say someone unexpectedly quit, or the company is growing faster than they anticipated. You know who is bogged down from all the extra work? The hiring manager. Or maybe the work isn't getting done and whose reputation is on the line? Management. Trust me, they want to make this work.

And of course you want to be hired. Really, everyone wants this interview to go well.

Your experience is flexible—their needs are probably not. How can you fit yourself into what they need? (And then decide if that's what you want.)

It's also possible, as you learn their needs, that it's not a match. And that's OK, but let that be your decision by gathering as much information as you can.

It's important to listen to what they say (and what they don't say). I approach interviews as "fact-finding missions". Be interested, be jovial, show your best side, but be discerning. After all, you are fabulous and have options. Asking questions also shows that you are interested and you care.

If you want to know what you'll actually do each day...

✗ DON'T ASK...
What's the day to day of this job?

> Why not? Because it's easy for someone to brush off that question by saying, "There is no day to day! It's wild here!" And there you are, left with nothing.

✓ ASK INSTEAD...
Wow, this job sounds really dynamic. If you had to assign a percentage to each of the job functions, what would that look like?

That will make them think, and then you can decide if that percentage break down is one that excites you. Remember, it's your call if you want to move forward.

✓ ALSO ASK...
Why is this role open now? How do you envision the company/position evolving in the next 3–5 years?

After they answer this question for you, wait a beat. They will say more, and you'll get a lot of additional context here.

This is an important question because they might say the job has new skill sets they haven't had before, or they realize they need an ABC type person on the team, or they want to grow the company in a certain direction, or there is so much work to do…their answer will help you get a better idea of the workload and expectations this role would have.

If you want to know about growth opportunities...

✗ DON'T ASK...
How challenging is this job? Is it going to be too easy? Will I get bored?

✓ **ASK INSTEAD...**
It seems like this role is pivotal to the organization. How would you describe the cross-functional interaction?

✓ **OR ASK...**
How much exposure does this role have to other teams and to the leadership team?

> **Here's why:** If the role gets you a lot of exposure to other teams, that might make it more possible for you to get a promotion or transfer departments if the job is too boring.

✓ **OR ASK...**
Where do you feel the biggest gaps exist within the team/company/organization and how does this role fulfill those?

> **Here's why:** When they answer this, if you have the experience they mention they are lacking, it's a great opportunity to casually say so. If you don't, you can say that you are interested in developing that way (if that's true of course). Connect the dots for them!

✗ **DON'T ASK...**
When do I get a raise?

✓ ASK INSTEAD...
How is success measured in this role?

> **Here's why:** If you anticipate that the compensation is going to be lower, you want to figure out how specifically they have mapped out promotion tracks for the role.

✓ OR ASK...
What personality traits do you think the most successful people here possess?

> If you have any of those, mention them—not in a braggy way though! You can say, "That's great to hear that you are looking for someone who is able to create structure. In my last role, I led a new project that our company hadn't done before...I was responsible for XYZ and it was a great learning experience."

✓ OR ASK...
I'm always looking to become a better professional. What is the path for growth in this role?

> **Listen to their answer**—do you like what they said? If you don't like the job you would have if you got a promotion there, do you think you will like the one you are interviewing for?

If you have concerns about team/company culture/work-life balance...

✗ DON'T ASK...
So why are your Glassdoor reviews so bad?

> Questions with a negative put people on the defense. And they make the hiring manager think, you, in turn, are a negative person.

✓ ASK INSTEAD...
I've seen on Glassdoor that people have said there's room to improve the company's work/life balance. What steps is leadership taking to address those concerns?

> **Here's why:** They get a chance to explain themselves. If they say they are doing a lot to correct the problem, you know they are at least making an effort to listen to employees. If they aren't doing anything, well, their silence to that question is pretty loud.

✓ OR ASK...
What do you like about working here?

> **Here's why:** People love talking about themselves.

✓ **OR ASK...**
(If it's an HR representative) *What do you think makes this company a place where people love to work?*

✓ **OR ASK...**
Why do you think people stay here after so many years?

✓ **OR ASK...**
(If it's the manager of your team) *Why do you think the team you've managed has been so successful?*

✓ **OR ASK...**
(If it's the manager of your team) *What's been your biggest challenge in managing a team—either at this company or at another?*

> **Here's why:** You will get insights into their management style, and you'll see how humble they are if they can admit their challenges.

If you want to know the compensation for the job...

✗ **DON'T ASK...**
How much does this pay?

✓ INSTEAD...
Wait for them to bring it up. If the first interview goes by, and they don't mention it, don't ask. Wait until you are further along in the process.

> **Here's why:** Remember—first round interviews are to gain a surface understanding of the job. If they provide a salary range, great. If not, asking first makes you come across as money-hungry and like you want the job for the wrong reasons. I know you need the salary question answered in order to move forward, but trust me...wait. (more to come on this in Chapter 5)

If you are in the final stage of the interview process, and you know everything you need to know and REALLY want the job...

✗ DON'T SAY...
Give me this job. I don't care what we need to do to make this work. I'll take anything!

✓ ASK INSTEAD...

(again—only in a final round interview) ***I'm really excited about the opportunity to use what I know and learn and grow with the team and the organization. If I were to come on board, what would you recommend I do between now and a potential start date - familiarize myself with software, read XYZ books, take an online training, etc.***

> I had a hiring manager call me to say they were deciding between their candidate and a candidate I was working with. The hiring manager told me that my candidate asked the question above and she was so impressed with her eagerness, that she hired her pretty much on the spot. If you mean it, it can work for you!

✎ EXERCISE

Practice your questions and answers in the mirror. This is something candidates laugh at when I suggest it...but then have come back to me after accepting a job. They say it works. It worked for me too when I was a candidate.

What else did you notice about these sample questions? **They weren't yes or no questions.**

★   **Extra credit:** Try going one day (OK, 3 hours) without asking a single yes or no question to someone. It's so hard! But note how much more you learn. If you want to make an informed decision about whether or not to accept a job or move forward in the interview process, you need as much detailed information as possible.

How to Answer Typical Tricky Interview Questions

"Tell me about yourself."

Chapter 1, you guyzzz! Leverage that elevator pitch like you've never leveraged anything in your life.

"Why did you leave your last job?" OR "Why are you looking for a new role?"

There is a distinction between these two questions: one is more negative-sounding than the other and will put you on the defense.

You never want to speak negatively about any employer you've ever had (even if they were terrible—and I'm sure you've got some stories in the vault—a job interview is not the time to share those!)

You end your answer to these questions the same way: explaining not only why you are open to a new role, but why this specific job is "the answer" you've been looking for.

For example, let's say I'm a recruiter who has only worked on the agency side, but now I'm looking to move into corporate recruiting.

"Why did you leave your last job?"

I truly enjoyed my last role, and learned a lot about the mechanics of recruiting and working with clients. I'd love to bring those skills to your company and also expand the range of roles for which I recruit. I know your company is putting an additional focus on financial recruiting, and I'd love to work in that vertical, which wasn't an opportunity in my previous company unfortunately. With my background working in the financial space, coupled with my recruiting experience, I believe it would be a great fit—challenging, yet also a way to capitalize on my previous experience.

"Why are you looking for a new role?"

I'm enjoying my role currently, but when the opportunity arose to interview with your company, I had to jump at the chance. I've been thinking it would be an amazing experience to recruit more in the financial space, and potentially other areas beyond what I'm doing now, which is why this role stood out to me.

NEVER say you've outgrown your current role. Hiring managers will think you will outgrow this new role too.

"What do you like about this industry?"

Of course this will depend on you. Always be honest in interviews. You don't have to provide a ton of extraneous information, but outside of it being unethical, lying about your skill set and interests could get you stuck doing a job you don't enjoy or one in which you're set up to fail.

I would say:

I love recruiting because, fundamentally, I believe in people. I grew up around hardworking people beating the odds and succeeding, so I know anyone can do it. I've seen it.

I'm great at encouraging and coaching others, and recruiting is a perfect way for me to do that in a one-on-one setting with candidates. I also enjoy learning about business and helping clients and/or internal stakeholders figure out the skill sets and personalities that will serve their company and drive revenue. In my last role, I exceeded my annual revenue goal by nearly 200%, while working with companies across industries, and roles that spanned from entry-level all the way up to C-level executives. I'd love to work at your company, so I can be inspired by my colleagues and attract others to be part of this experience.

End your answer with something specific about the uniqueness of their company.

"Why do you want to work here?"

Think about your **WHY**. Do you believe in the company's mission, were you inspired by the work of their leadership team, were their online reviews good, did you hear about the company in the news or from a friend? Do you really not care and just need to pay bills? (If this last one is true, do your best in climbing out of that mindset, and find something about the company that is interesting.)

Your passion needs to come through in the interview.

"What do you know about our company?"

Chapter 2—you've done your prep work, so you know what to do here!

Explain this gap in your resume.

First of all, if you have a gap in your resume, don't freak out about it. Think about what happened. Did you get laid off/fired? Did you take care of a family member? If so, think about anyone at your last job (preferably your manager or someone on the leadership team) who could serve as a professional reference.

If you were laid off, you could say something like:

I really enjoyed my last job and learned [XYZ skills that are applicable to this job you're interviewing for]. Unfortunately, they had a reduction in force and my role was affected. That said, I have references from the company who could speak to my performance there, and I'd be happy to put you in touch.

If it was a medical reason, you could say:

I enjoyed my previous role, but unfortunately, there were some medical issues in my family, and I needed to take a leave of absence to care for them. If you'd like to speak with someone at my previous company regarding my performance, I'd be happy to put you in touch. Or if you need me to take extra testing to make sure my skills are still sharp, I'm happy to do that as well.

"What is your desired salary?"

The first time they ask you this, say:

I'm interested in the entire compensation package, and if this role ends up being something that's a great fit, I'm sure I'd be excited about whatever the offer would be.

At that point, they will either be happy and give you the range. Or they will follow up with:

"That's great, but how much are you looking for?"

Some companies have flexibility with compensation and some do not. So don't be squirrely. Give a range. You can say:

"Ideally, I'm seeking around [provide your reasonable salary range that you would accept within 10–20K, with the lowest amount you

would accept at the bottom of the range], which seems to be in line with what I'm seeing in the market. However, if you're sitting on a million dollars back there, I'll take that too."

Salary conversations are serious, so if you can bring some levity, it shows that money is not your primary motivation.

✎ EXERCISE

You guessed it. Practice these answers in the mirror or with a friend.

★ **Extra credit:** Record yourself! If you have practiced your answers for these questions, you will feel less nervous during your interview.

You've got your interview questions for the day-of all set. Now, let's go to Chapter 4 to talk about interview etiquette and proper follow up strategy.

CHAPTER 4:
Interview Etiquette

"Almost everyone will make a good first impression, but only a few will make a good lasting impression."

– Sonya Parker

I have some shocking news for you. Your interview starts as soon as a company reaches out to you, or as soon as you apply for the job.

Wait, what?! They haven't even met me yet.

Oh yes, they have. And that's a good thing. They have your contact information, and maybe your resume, and they've creeped on your social media, and...they want to know more! (Hopefully your social media is family-friendly!)

Recruiters and hiring managers are of course checking initially for those hard skills we discussed. Now they want to know how easy you are to work with, and, equally important, how you can make their lives easier.

Here are some tips and rules for interview etiquette:

Corresponding with the Hiring Team

Make it easy for them!

- If they email you to set up time for an interview, re-attach your resume (even though they already have it). That way they can easily forward it on to others instead of having to hunt for it.

- Include your contact information at the bottom of your email (I know it's on your resume that you've attached, but what if they can't open the attachment, or someone forgets to forward it, etc.?) Make it easy!

- Proofread, proofread, proofread! Write an email, save it and come back to it in an hour if you have to. If your email is riddled with errors, they will assume you have low attention to detail.

Phone Interview Etiquette

I'm taking a leap here and assuming your phone has caller ID. If you are on the job search and you don't recognize the phone number, **always** answer your phone in an "interview voice". My go to is, with a smile, *"Hi, this is Jenna."* That way if it's the dentist confirming my appointment, it's friendly enough.

You never know who could be calling. I had a recruiter call me about a job four months after I applied! I was driving and I was not hands-free, so I said, *"Oh, thank you for your call. It's great to hear from you! I'm driving right now but I can pull over—can you hold on for just one moment?"* Try to keep them on the line, because sometimes it is hard to get a hold of them again!

On the flip side as a recruiter, I've cold-called many candidates.

I had one gal answer the phone with *"Yeah?"*. This same candidate flushed the toilet during our phone interview. Maybe she does her best thinking there, but I'm just glad it wasn't a video interview!

Respect people's time. If the interview is scheduled for 30 minutes, but it's going really well and not ready to wrap up, say something about 28 minutes into it, like, *"I know we are coming up on time...do you have a few more minutes?"*

People appreciate that consideration, and usually do have extra time. Or, they will tell you they have to wrap it up. At that point, you can either ask them what the next steps are, or ask if they would prefer to schedule more time with you at their convenience.

In-person Interview Etiquette

- Arrive 10 minutes early. I have had candidates who are so conscientious, they go as far as doing a practice drive/train ride a few days before. If that makes you less nervous on interview day, then do it!

- Bring copies of your resume. Always. I probably should've titled this book *Bring Copies of Your Resume* because really folks...it's that important and it's such a simple thing!

- Don't take it personally if (when) your interviewers are late to start your interview. You never know what they had going on that day.

- Don't get rattled when they change the schedule, location, interviewee list on you.

- Roll with it! If someone tells you something crazy, roll with it. If it's a virtual in-person interview, and you're on a Zoom video call and the cat climbs on top of your interviewer, don't let it throw you off your game. You don't have to like everything you hear, but don't blow your chances on a great opportunity just because the interview process doesn't go exactly as you would expect. Neither will your job.

- Don't hog the conversation. Remember the strategy—ask open-ended questions.

> **Reminder:** We are talking about how you should behave, but throughout the process, I want you to put in the back of your mind how they behave. Do they call when they say they will? Are they giving you a good candidate experience? When it's offer time, this will come back to you and we will discuss it in Chapter 5.

Thank You Note Rules

The purpose of a thank you note is to show gratitude, right? Partly, yes. It's nice that they spent time with you, but the real reason for writing a thank you note is actually to reiterate your interest in the job and drive the interview process forward.

In terms of note etiquette, these are my rules. You may not agree, but have you ever been passed over for a job because you were *too* polite? I didn't think so.

- If it's a phone interview, an email thank you note is fine. Six sentences and send it within 24 hours after your interview.

- For an in-person interview, a short emailed thank you note is fine within 24 hours, and I also do a more personalized handwritten note. Sometimes you might be interviewing at a large corporation where people do not get their mail very quickly. So you can bring your thank you notes with you to your interview, and then right after it's over, sit in the lobby and write the notes and then ask the receptionist to give the notes to your interviewers.

- Sometimes you are interviewed by several people at once. Each person should receive an individual and different note.

- If everyone works remotely, you may just want to stick with email thank you notes. It is sort of weird before you get a job to mail a thank you note to someone's personal address.

- Send a thank you after every interview round, and make them different, because each interview is different.

- If you don't get their contact information, make sure you write down their full name and then message them a thank you note on LinkedIn (aren't you resourceful!), and add them as a connection.

Check your spelling and grammar. *"Jenna, who WOULDN'T do that?!"* You would think I don't need to say this. But, I've found typos in 99% of the thousands of thank you notes that I've seen. One time, a candidate (applying to a communications role) had so many typos in her thank you note, the client decided not to consider her for the job. They said, *"If this candidate writes a thank you note with this many errors, how is she going to communicate with media on behalf of our company?"* Solid point.

Remember—every part of the process is the interview—how you answer your phone, how you act in the elevator, how you talk to the receptionist, how you wait in the waiting room, how you behave as you walk out, how you follow up...do you need me to keep going? Bring copies of your resume.

> **Side note**: If you are an employer, make sure to tell your employees that candidates are coming into the office to interview. Here's why:

I had a candidate show up for an interview with my client. She was sitting by the entrance (10 minutes early like we discussed!) and overheard employees talking about how horrible the company was. They were just openly speaking so negatively. They were frustrated about the company's business strategy, didn't think leadership was competent, etc. The candidate said the interview, once it started, was fine, but she had concerns from overhearing the previous conversation. She didn't move forward in the process.

Interview Follow Up

Don't be afraid to follow up with your interviewers if you don't get a response (and don't get discouraged). At the end of your interview, it's always good to reiterate your interest in the role and say, *"What do you envision for next steps?"* A lot of times, the interviewers will say, *"We'll know more after the holidays, or we will contact you next week, our VP is on vacation until Friday, if you don't hear from us, reach out on the 15th, etc..."*

I would say if they tell you they'll know more next week, you can follow up after 2 weeks. But you have to be strategic in your follow up. Use your follow up to drive the process forward (just like the purpose of your thank you note).

Don't you hate it when people leave you a voicemail and just say "call me back"?! So infuriating. Emailing someone "just to check in" produces the same sentiment.

- Follow up every 2 weeks up to three times. After that, keep going with your search and they'll call you when they call you.

- In your follow up, reiterate what you are excited about and why you think you would be a strong candidate—but remember, don't ramble!

- After your second follow up, you can put a timeline on it and say, "*Would you like me to follow up next week in case we aren't able to connect?*" That will show your persistence, and asking a question elicits a response. On their end, a number of things can happen that have nothing to do with you. Sometimes people really do get busy, or they make an offer to a candidate who declines, they change the requirements of the job, the hiring manager gets promoted or leaves, funding they anticipated falls through...most of the reason for the silent treatment has nothing to do with you.

- Be strategic about your time of day and week for your follow ups. Don't send the email on a Saturday or late at night. Tuesday or Wednesday mornings are good times because they could get back to you the same day and they are less likely to be on a vacation.

You can say something like:

I really have enjoyed meeting the team over the past couple of weeks and discussing the marketing manager opportunity. I believe I would be a great fit, given my financial industry experience, my success with running marketing automation platforms, and scaling marketing programs over the last four years. Are there any other questions about my experience that I can answer for you or the team? I'd welcome the opportunity to move forward in the process and I'm also happy to share professional references if you'd like.

All the best,

[Your Name]

[Phone Number]

[Email—even though you emailed them and you know they have your information!—make it easy!!!]

✎ EXERCISES

(Pick two or do them all for Extra Credit!)

- If your interview is in person, do a practice run to the office.

- Practice interviewing with a friend or someone who is critical/opinionated/helpful.

- Practice in front of the mirror.

- If your interview is on video, make sure you practice using your technology and that you are in a place where you get strong cell phone service/internet, there's good lighting, a suitable background, you know where your camera is and where to look into it, etc.

So you are done with your interview process and now it's time for the big show...the offer stage! Head to Chapter 5 and we'll get into it!

CHAPTER 5:
What to Know Before Accepting an Offer

"If we're always guided by other people's thoughts, what's the point of having our own?"
— Oscar Wilde

You're in the home stretch, and they're about to make it official. You've got the offer in hand. Great! Now, let's take a look.

Questions to Consider as You Weigh Your Offer

- Did you get all of your questions answered?
- Do you understand what the job is/will be?
- Are you interested in this job and able to succeed in it?
- Is it clear how to succeed in this job?

- Have you had transparent conversations about salary and are you happy with those?

- Have you taken into account the other benefits they offer?

Never accept an offer on the spot. Even if it is amazing, you still need to sleep on it and talk to your family or any other relevant parties. That said, some offers do expire after 48 hours or up to a week, so you need to make somewhat of a timely decision.

When considering an offer, here are some questions to ask yourself:

How desperate are you?

It's OK to say "very" (to me, not to them!) but be honest. You've got bills and obligations and nothing else coming close to being an offer. I made a career pivot to an entry level recruiting job at age 31, and they offered me a salary that was waaaay lower than what I made in my PR job. I told myself it was going to essentially be like going back to school and I was "paying my tuition". I vowed to grind every day until I learned the job and could ask for a raise or find another higher paying job. The offer was low, but it was fair because I was going to gain valuable experience. And, they had more leverage than I did at the time.

How desperate are they?

Maybe they need all hands on deck, and that means you might have more leverage than you think. Or they need someone with very specific and rare experience, which you have. I wouldn't try to take advantage of that leverage (some people might tell you to) but I'm a firm believer in doing great work and the promotions, money, fame, glory, recognition, good vibes, etc. will come. For instance, if they need you to start right away, maybe you can say, *"That would be wonderful! I'm so excited to join the company! That said, I'm unable to start in the office until October 1st, so if you want me to start in September, I'd likely need to work remotely for those first few weeks."*

This happens sometimes when people are relocating for a job, or if they've been unemployed and need time to figure out childcare, or they want their kids to finish out the school year in the same school, sell their house, etc.

Are you happy with the proposed salary?

The salary they are offering should not be a surprise at this point, because you've provided a consistent range throughout the interview process.

> *I had a candidate who was interviewing for a sales role at a technology company. She told me she wanted $90,000, but during*

her interview, she told the CEO she wanted $120,000. When he and I were discussing the candidate, the salary inconsistency came up. Immediately, he was concerned with the validity of her experience and wondered what else she could be hiding. Not a good way to make an impression! The interview process was cut short pretty much right after that, because she made a smaller mistake and he was already on the lookout for additional inconsistencies.

Is the salary higher than you wanted?

And you loved everything about the interviewing experience and the job? You're ready to sign!

Is the salary lower than you wanted?
OK, ask yourself:

- **Did you see that coming?** Were they transparent about that? *"We are a startup and we pay below market unfortunately."*

- **Did you ask for too much?** One time a gal asked me what "she was worth". I told her, *"My mom would say you are worth a million dollars, but the market rate for the position you are seeking is between $105,000–120,000."*

- **Is there anything else you really need that would make up the difference?** I had a candidate receive an offer with a lower salary than he wanted. They were transparent from the get-go, and he really wanted the job. It was outside the city and he needed a car, so we were able to negotiate a stipend that covered payments and car insurance to make it work for him. If you feel the offer is lower than what you want, another thing you can do is ask them to include a clause in the employment contract/offer letter that says after 6 months of employment they will revisit your salary if you meet XYZ requirements (which you can determine with them).

- **What about the "Hidden Paycheck?"** Benefits, take home pay, vacation… (back to your deal breakers from Chapter 1). If the salary is lower, do the benefits make up for that? And are they benefits you would actually benefit from?

- **What are the other non-financial perks?** Maybe you absolutely loved everyone there and you could tell they enjoyed being at work everyday, or you know the schedule is good, you can walk to the office instead of driving, you're going to learn a new skill, you can bring your dog…If you can pay your bills and have an easier life, is that worth it for you?

DISCLAIMER: Those are my personal success stories on negotiating offers. There are plenty of resources that will help you with negotiations. I'm not a negotiation expert.

I also want to reiterate that it's important to pay attention to the way the company behaves throughout the interview process. Do they make decisions quickly? That can be an indicator of a company that's not afraid to innovate and take risks. Do they follow up with you when they say they will?

Throughout your interviews, it is a good idea to make a mental note of how you feel you're being treated during the process.

Listen to your gut.

Conclusion

Didn't get the job?

It happens! I've also missed out on what I thought was the *dream job*. I know that doesn't make you feel better because it doesn't change your situation, but it's important to remember that the job search and the interview process are existential exercises. Through this interview process, you've learned about yourself, your deal breakers, what to look for in a company, and you are all the wiser for it.

I interviewed for a soft drink company, and I had three interviews with them, met the whole PR team, and I gave what I thought were great answers to their questions and the job seemed right up my alley. I didn't have food and beverage PR experience, but I had crisis experience and hospitality experience, which I believe would have transferred well. I followed up, multiple times, and never heard anything. I was really disappointed, because I thought I did everything right. That said, if I had gotten that job, I never would have gotten my next awesome job, which led me to recruiting, which led me to cultivate a skillset that I love, and I believe I can ultimately help more people this way. It took me three years to realize the silver lining.

You've gotta keep trying. It only takes one right match to change your life. The fact that you are reading content like this shows your commitment to sharpening your skills and shows your work ethic. I know others will see what a valued employee you will be. Keep your head up. Your time will come.

You can also ask the interviewing team/HR for feedback. Sometimes, they realize they need a different type of experience, or they want someone with management experience. Or they need someone to start right away, and that is incompatible with your schedule. The worst that can happen is they don't give you any feedback. But if you keep asking each company, and hear the same things over again, it's a good idea to look inward and see how you can improve or maybe apply for a different type of role.

Just because that specific position didn't work out, that doesn't mean the door is closed to future opportunities there. One of my best friends interviewed for **fourteen** positions at the same company. She was eventually hired, and stayed there for 10 years and got promoted several times.

I had one candidate who didn't get the job, but our client loved him. Three months later, they were growing and opened another similar role, and asked him to come back and get on board with them. It's all about timing and finding the right fit.

✎ FINAL EXERCISE

Write down everything you've learned from this experience, adapt, and most importantly, keep going.

You Got The Job?

Congratulations! Now, fortunately and unfortunately, the real work starts. Read up on as much as you can before your start date, familiarize yourself with any software, and get ready to dominate and take charge of your new role on Monday morning!

Also, take some time to thank any of your contacts for helping you land an interview, telling you about a job, etc. A simple call, text or email to say thanks and to update them on your search goes a long way. And you never know if they could help you again!

Remember, regardless of what happens in your interview: ABN—Always Be Networking.

Network the most when you need it the least.

Networking is just one letter away from "not working".

How many clever sayings do you need?

Opportunities can come from anywhere. I have met great candidates on the bus and at playing card tournaments. I met my last boss at a conference in Las Vegas. I got an internship through a professor's former student.

So keep your eyes open and your confidence up!

Good luck!

Acknowledgements

This goes out to the candidates I've helped over the years. Thank you for giving me the OOMPH to articulate my interviewing philosophy into a book. I truly believe we have all the pieces, and sometimes we just need a little guidance on putting them all together. I hope this can help whoever reads this!

Also, a big thank you to my proofreaders—Jenna (not me, different Jenna), Neil, Ryan, Pat and Sal.

And a special shout out to my husband for his unconditional support and exemplary design skills.

About the author

Jenna Kimball is a recruiter and former marketing professional who's coached thousands of candidates through the job interview process. Formerly a board member of the Chicago American Marketing Association and the National Practitioners Council where she gave job interview advice to their national membership base, Jenna has been featured on webinars and panel discussions about how people can achieve success early in their careers. She has extensive experience working with marketing candidates across a variety of industries, from first-time job seekers to senior executives. Jenna lives in Chicago with her family.